STORIES OF AN ENTREPRENEUR EXTRAORDINAIRE

"ENTREPRENEUR LESSONS"

OF

MADAME FOUNDER

By Yolanda R. Lamar
The Entrepreneur Extraordinaire

STORIES OF AN
ENTREPRENEUR EXTRAORDINAIRE

"Entrepreneur Lessons of Madame Founder"

Written by Yolanda R. Lamar

Houston, Texas

HATCHBACK Publishing

Stories of an Entrepreneur Extraordinaire
Entrepreneur Lessons of Madame Founder
© 2012 by Yolanda R. Lamar

All rights reserved. This book is protected under the copyright laws of the United States of America. No part of this book may be reproduced or transmitted in any form or by any means without written permission from the author or publisher.

Unless otherwise noted all definitions are taken from dictionary.com

Published and Cover Design By:
HATCHBACK Publishing
Genesee, Michigan 48437

ISBN 978-1479184637

For Worldwide Distribution
Printed in the U.S.A.

Acknowledgments

I am so deeply indebted to some people for important infrastructure contributions to this book. Others I am indebted to for important ideas. Others I am indebted to for specific illustrations. Others were supporters or mentors. A special thanks goes out to Valerie Southall of Flint, Michigan who planted the internal seed of "you need to write this book" concept. She saw the vision of me writing this book early on and I appreciate her sharing her thoughts. I would also like to thank one of my Male Mentors who blessed me with the entitlement of "Entrepreneur Extraordinaire with long hair" many, many years ago, Mr. Cortes Everett. He continues to this day to grace me with this entitlement every time we talk.

I would like to extend special thanks to my HERO, Mr. Charles Wilder who God only knows came into my life and expanded by entrepreneurial horizons in so many ways of which if it wasn't for his love and support of seeing and believing in the potentials of my entrepreneurial growth, I wouldn't be here to share my lessons of love as a true entrepreneur. Thanks Big Guy!

And last but definitely not least, to my Momma, Lottie Ruth Hamler who truly without even knowing continues to love, support and care for me no matter what.

I really do love you all for supporting me and being that backbone of love and encouragement during my entrepreneurial growth now and beyond and Thank you God for the Gift of Favor to your Daughter!

*An **"Entrepreneur Extraordinaire"** provides and offers valuable tools to help you plan, clarify and create a significantly successful business, while being an extraordinary individual at the same time.*

En·tre·pre·neur ~ [ahn-truh-pruh-nur, -noor;]
an enterprising individual who builds capital through risk and/or initiative. [1][note 1]

ex·tra·or·di·naire ~ [ĕk'strə-ôr'dn-âr', -dē-nâr']
beyond what is ordinary or usual; highly unusual or exceptional or remarkable;

Check this out!
↓

Table of Contents

Foreword

Introduction

In the Beginning Entrepreneur	Chapter 1
Exploratory Entrepreneur	Chapter 2
Moving Toward Xtraordinary	Chapter 3
Extraordinaire Beginnings	Chapter 4
History of Being Extraordinaire	Chapter 5
The Entrepreneur Extraordinaire Herself	Chapter 6
Networking Extraordinaire	Chapter 7
Building Relationships Extraordinaire	Chapter 8
So Who Are They?	Chapter 9
Story of Women Entrepreneurs of America	Chapter 10

Forward

Yolanda Lamar-Wilder knows just about everything there is to know about starting and sustaining a business as an entrepreneur. In this book, she shares her knowledge with you.

She takes all of her experiences, breaks it down to its' essence and then makes it practical. She will answer many questions a new entrepreneur may be asking (and questions you may not have thought to ask) and explain them in a way in which you can use and benefit.

Madame Founder, Yolanda Lamar-Wilder opens up her entrepreneurial life so that you can climb up and start building your business on a tried, true and firm foundation. That is what makes this book so exceptional.

The most important message in this book is that if you have that great desire to become a successful entrepreneur, you can do it. It is not necessarily easy but it can be done. Where do you go to get the right information? The solution is in your hands, all you need to do is read and turn the pages.

Cynthia L. Hatcher

She believed she could so she did

Introduction

The Stories of an Entrepreneur Extraordinaire, Lessons by Madame Founder is truly a book written with *true entrepreneurs* in mind. The story is about an Ordinary business woman who started out on a shoe-string budget in starting her business and realized she was an Extraordinary Entrepreneur in supporting and empowering more women in sharing about her *entrepreneurial path.*

I was told just recently that I was a good storyteller so I was encouraged to write this book to share about my entrepreneurial path of how it all became and its manifestation to where I am now. Fifteen years in the making of trials, tribulations, the high and low roads, the success stories, the conversations, the plans, the process, the education, the wisdom and teachings that comes with being a successful entrepreneur in this world today.

Never, I mean never, in my wildest imagination did I ever dream that I would be writing a book about my life as *"being an entrepreneur."* You or nobody that looked like you could have given me a crystal ball that would have told me, "You will be writing a book about your entrepreneurial path."

I would have not believed it or you.

I had incorporated early in my mind that when you step out in starting your own business that an entrepreneur is a "spirit", a spirit of being in business for yourself. So, with coming from Corporate America myself after 15+ years, when the opportune time was planted for me to step out on faith in starting my own business, all I knew was my spirit led me to start a business. It wasn't a need to start one. I was blessed to be surrounded by mentors who spoke and encouraged the idea but was truly blessed to be married to an "entrepreneur" at that time who encouraged me as well to start my own business. Now I know there are many of you out there that want to start a business but don't have that support system in place but it shouldn't change that you have the spirit of entrepreneurship which has ignited in you and now you are ready to get started. So now the question is where to start?

I pray this book will assist and empower many who are challenged or maybe moving in the direction of the spirit of entrepreneurship and feel propelled to move forward after reading my book. The lessons I've learned were and are very vivid and real to say the least. I write to encourage the reader to see the spirit of the author. The beauty of entrepreneurship is the concept of many facets. My goal here is to share what is relevant and what is expected in starting and sustaining a business in this economy.

With me starting my entrepreneurial path over 15 years ago, trust and believe me, a lot has changed. Some, for the good and much for the worst because of the recession that set so many large corporations back, putting thousands and thousands of people out of work. So as I watch this trend explode, I asked questions of many who felt stuck, "Have you considered starting your own business? What are you good at? Do you have any skills or trade that would help get a business started? What is it that you did for XYZ Company that you could implement in supporting yourself?" I mean, these are questions that I felt warranted in getting your mind running, rejuvenated and brainstorm some ideas. Let it flow!

With someone who has started several businesses of my own, I will be sharing stories to enlighten you on your entrepreneur path and educate you of the many lessons taught and learned. I am a true believer in sharing the wealth of knowledge. The seed of acknowledgment in knowing everyone needs that supportive service in being in business for themselves. You need these stories of how to, why and what to get to the next level. I believe sharing is caring and as you well know, it's about the power of knowing that gets you where you need to be.

I pray this book assist your challenges, your expectations and revelations of being an entrepreneur. Remember, it's the spirit of being an entrepreneur that will help you grow and sustain that business you so want to start. My personal and business lessons may not ever affect you or you may never run into some of the bumps in the road of starting and running your business, but this book will lay some nuggets of inspiration and showcase the dedication of the author's passion in being "An Entrepreneur Extraordinaire."

My wish for you after you read the Stories of An Entrepreneur Extraordinaire that you too can accomplish whatever your heart desires in starting and running that dream business and having a support system in place.
Get Empowered! Be Extraordinaire!

She turned her can'ts into cans, and her dreams into plans.

Chapter 1

In the Beginning Entrepreneur

"You can't share if you haven't been through it"

There's a story to be shared and one that will accommodate your curiosity of what is an Entrepreneur Extraordinaire! Amazingly enough, it taken some time to share but now, it's about to be revealed because the powers to be says it is so. You can only share your life's journeys and what you've experienced. Sometimes the measurement of outcome does and will help someone else who is traveling through that same or similar journey. I want to make you feel right at home while you sit and read through the thoughts, pictures and quotes shared with me, some by me and some shared by others.

Take a load off, it has been a great journey so far, but the road ahead is just beginning for my life as a true entrepreneur. I really want you to enjoy my book and envision the life of being an "Entrepreneur Extraordinaire" and of my mission and purpose for my entrepreneurial world. I want you to get comfortable and enjoy my book and as you come to the close of this reading, I would love some feedback of your journey here with me.

For those of you that don't know, I was born and raised in Gary, Indiana by parents, Eurell Lamar and Lottie R. Hamler. I was the youngest daughter and the quiet one too. I grew up in a well-rounded, family-oriented circle. My maternal grandmother, Mary E. Hamler, was truly the matriarch of our family. We always had family gatherings and connected well with each other. Cousins were like sisters and brothers in our family. It was truly a village in our family as I was growing up.

Amazingly to share, I used to love to write when I was in school, putting dibble-dabble all in the school books. It's a wonder they didn't send my parents a bill for all of the "art" I had done. Just writings such as "an ocean of thoughts and dreams" about me and my high school boyfriend and where I saw my life when I grew up. But now, I don't like writing as much. Wonder why? I was very active in school, yes I was. Involved in many after-school programs and upon entering high school, I enrolled in ROTC and served on the Drill Team for at least three years and many Home Economics cooking programs. I was

very active indeed. School was going well for me as a young girl until I got involved with a young man and the ultimate situation happened to me. Yes, yes, yes, I got pregnant. Yes, my story is very similar to many other young girls who don't stay focused. Well, my story is truly *"you-nique"* indeed because I got re-focused and expeditiously too. God blessed me with a beautiful baby boy first and I graduated with my class from Gary Theodore J. Roosevelt High School.

With staying focused, life became very realistic very quickly, so I enrolled at a Community College in Gary, Indiana and received my Secretarial Science certificate of which I was a Certified Secretary, didn't you know that reader? And during that time of educational growth, guess what? I was blessed to have a daughter along the way.

Well, it was quite clear that I wasn't going to grow and fulfill my American dream in Gary, Indiana so we, speaking 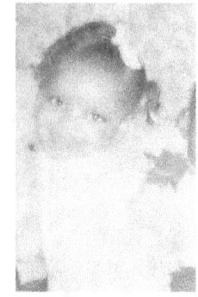 father of the kids, the kids and I packed up and relocated to Denver, Colorado. We were encouraged by a good friend of my Mom's that this would be the environment for a young couple to raise and grow their family. So moving on to a better life away and guess what? As we arrived and got settled, I enrolled in Platt

College in Aurora, Colorado for Business Administration in receiving my Associates of which another child was blessed to arrive. Amazingly enough I completed my schooling and received my Associates Degree and began my studies as a Paralegal and received my certification which truly sparked my entrepreneurial path.

So let's recap. *In the beginning*, my entrepreneurial travels growing up steered me towards from moving from Gary, Indiana, relocating to Denver, Colorado with the kids' father after graduation. From there to Indianapolis, Indiana, then to Cleveland, Ohio then back to Indianapolis, Indiana with three children (Steve Jr., Shavon and Shawn Sr.) who are now grown with children of their own. I now have eleven grandchildren who are a part of this expanding family all living in Indianapolis, Indiana. So now the saga begins! Those close to her call her...

"Peaches"

Lesson:
How did your entrepreneurial introduction begin? "Trust me there is a beginning to it."

Chapter 2

Exploratory Entrepreneur

"Give a man a fish, and you'll feed him for a day. Teach a man to fish, and he will eat for a lifetime."

As I begin this exploratory journey as a start up entrepreneur, I have so much to share and so much for which to be thankful and appreciative. As I play back in my mind to what to share with you, it was never a thought of mine to start and run a business. I've always since college, worked and worked hard as a waitress/server, retail/cashiering positions, supervisory positions in the food chain, law enforcement position in the prison system and human resource management/recruiter. I also was in the transportation industry such as a driver for a school system, drove a truck locally and as a chauffeur for supplemental income to feed my family. In having all these employment experiences under my belt, it allowed and gave me the tools and knowledge to position me where I am today. Now, again, never in my wildest dreams did I ever think about starting a business of my own. What? Who? Me?

Lesson:

Explore your entrance into entrepreneurship by starting documenting/journaling about your thoughts and dreams when they become vivid.

So as these nuggets were being placed, I wasn't moving my feet progressively as I should have been. Why? Because I wasn't tuned into my "exploratory entrepreneurial tunnel." You say, what's that? Well, I didn't know either, until I got "the pink slip" concept brought to me then that tunnel vision started to unwind and open expeditiously, but not quite as quickly. See if your circle of influences believes and know of your potential, they are the ones who will be sowing seeds into your "exploratory tunnel." I mean, there are really some folk who truly do want to see you go to the "next level" of what God has given you. You may not see it but there are a few if not many that will and those that are true to your existence, will share with you and encourage you. Trust me, start your exploratory *entrepreneurial thinking!*

Let's touch on this just a bit right here and right now!

Let's get those thoughts to moving. *"Some individuals hold either an entity theory of intelligence, known as a fixed mindset or an incremental theory of intelligence, known as a growth mindset. Individuals with a fixed mindset believes that one's intelligence abilities, talents and attributes are permanent and unchangeable. I further believe that one's ability comes from their talents, rather than from their slow development of skills through learning and as such giving up or declining in the face of setbacks. Individuals with an entrepreneurial mindset see needs, problems and challenges as opportunities and develop innovative ways to deal with them. I'm spotlighting this concept to help you comprehend the characteristics and important factors of an entrepreneurial exploratory mindset and to offer a self-assessment tool right here to explore the current mindset of entrepreneurs.*

So that started with me!

Lesson:

"Self-assess yourself!" Think back to when or if the "pink slip theory" happened to you and create your own exit to entrepreneurship strategy!

So let me share with you about the exploratory thinking of an entrepreneur, ME! Well during the planning stages intricately of my employment career, God was working on me with my exit entrepreneurial strategy. Now, I was never aware of it and really, who knows when you are truly gonna get the official pink slip unless you are truly a "piss-poor excuse of an employee" which in exchange you could never see yourself as a Entrepreneur Extraordinaire. I'm just sayin' right!

Well, there was this external nugget of a Business man by the name of Pil Kim. I will never, ever forget this individual. I mean, when I explored and assessed my entrepreneurial tunnel, I have to thank God for this gentleman. He was a true business extraordinaire who owned a few check cashing businesses in Cleveland, Ohio. He had been a client of mine in the employment industry. My actual last place of employment before start my own company was a local Clerical and Light Industrial Staffing Agency.

He was truly the one individual who "opened" my mind to entrepreneurship. Now, I want to make sure I send out a Special Thanks to my Ex-husband and business partner for so many years, Mr. Charles Wilder who too elevated me internally because he too was and is a true entrepreneur and businessman in the music/recording industry to this day. He was the internal nugget and "wind beneath me" who supported and guided me as I stepped out on faith to start my own business. Who? What? Me? Yes!

Stories of An Entrepreneur Extraordinaire

Pil Kim was truly instrumental in sharing with me on my talents and skills as a Recruiter in the Staffing industry. I had the job order to find him accountants for his new check cashing centers and trust me, he was a client with a no-nonsense disposition.

His requirements were truly challenging because I needed to place candidates who understood Chinese and spoke it fluently. Well, we had a well diversified staffing agency and it was so comforting to know that I could solidify his hiring needs. As I served him as a client of the staffing agency he saw something else in me that was just not about recruiting and employment. He always felt the need to schedule meetings after I placed candidates for his job order and unbeknownst to me, he didn't want to talk about the job order or the candidates, NO!

He always edified how great my customer service skills were and shared with the company of my great work ethics in placing the right candidates for his business. But these meetings were not about his employment candidates or the company, he wanted to talk about starting my own business in the staffing industry. What? To be quite frank and honest, we had at least four meetings. To make this story short, I never realized from the first meeting up until the third meeting of what his purpose of meeting with me was all about.

The first meeting was just setting the tone, a "picking my brain" type of meeting. Now I can see it. He asked many questions that a person of interest in wanting to start a business would ask of you. Believe me, my answers were not favorite ones because I had no desire to be an entrepreneur.

So he commenced to lay those "exploratory entrepreneurial nuggets" that I spoke about earlier in my hard head (laughing). The questions I remember him asking were like, "How do you like what you do for XYZ company? How familiar are you in the industry you work? What makes you qualified to be such a great recruiter in your industry?"

Well, my answers were probably similar to yours if you've been in the industry of choice for quite sometime. Yes, I loved what I did because I am a people-person and I positioned myself to learn as much of the industry to "craft" myself as a great recruiter. Well, he was alright with the answers but he shared with me on how important it was to seek the opportunity of what I have to offer and see how it would benefit me to start my own company. Yeah Right!

The next meeting was to present me with some documents of showcasing my talents on paper. He commenced to share the numbers theory about the company I worked for. Meaning, he wanted me to know my net worth with this company versus my skill level worth for this company. He shared their bottom line of business with his company of what I was bringing into their company. Meaning, I was not receiving my net worth for the kind of skill level I was bringing the company. He broke it down of what dollars I was making for XYZ company in servicing his business. It still wasn't clear to me on why he felt the need to share this but my *"exploratory mindset"* started to wander. Yes it did!

Lesson:
"Learn your craft and secure it!" You never know who is watching and what opportunities may come to fruition because of your knowledge.

Amazing enough by the third meeting, it was clearer to me of his purpose of "sharing these nuggets" with me and now it gets interesting to say the least.

I began to share information about these meetings with

my husband, Charles Wilder, and interesting enough, he was truly elated of the meetings and began to speak in "tongues" about the direction of these meetings. Charles continued to remind me of my worth and how it was not "far from sight" to see this. SEE WHAT?

I mean, Charles had already started and was running his recording studio/business and knew of the challenges. Now with me, all I ever did was worked for CEOs, Presidents and Executives in their businesses. I was very familiar with the "ends and outs" of the business world in starting up and what it took but why would I be thinking about starting my own with no monies. We were struggling with his business but he was sustaining it, a major difference. RIGHT! RIGHT!

Well, it's clearer more than ever by the fourth scheduled meeting of the "exploratory minds" that I am now considering going into business with Pil Kim in starting a new employment agency in Cleveland, Ohio. OH YEAH! I implemented the move by first bringing on a friend to the company I worked for, who was in need of a job. A person of interest who I shared and discussed these opportunities of stepping out on faith to get into the staffing industry as a business owner. She and I worked on several projects together in the past in the staffing industry and she was recently laid off from her job. So it made so much sense to hire her as my Assistant Recruiter at that time. I was excited about the meetings now but still wasn't clear on how to exit. Pil Kim pretty much had put a lot of thoughts to this prior to meeting with me, and of course, because he had an "operational plan" in the making for me to review. WHAT?

This operational plan was written out and explained clearly to me. I was then very clear of what I needed to do, where to start, the requirements of getting started and of course, the bottom line details on how the money should be accumulated. The last meeting allowed me to think about it, talk it over with my husband and allow me time to "exit" my current job when ready. REALLY?

Well, it didn't happen overnight readers, No it didn't! Because I continued to work for XYZ Staffing Agency for quite sometime but he and I stayed in touch. He was very encouraging but, also very persistent in knowing why I wasn't ready. Great question Pil Kim, but all I was thinking by now was, I don't have any money to start a new business. So after racking my brain on what I needed to do, you have no idea what was brewing behind my back. HA!

Remember the friend of all friends that I did much business work with and provided her a job when she was laid off? Yes, her! She was going behind my back and informing the boss at XYZ Staffing Agency of my exit plans. She literally had been sharing with the company CEOs and Directors of my meetings with Pil Kim on implementing my own Staffing Agency. YES SHE DID! She even made it appear that I was sharing company secrets of which we all know in the industry is a "no-no." That was so untrue. Now, the plans were to include her as a partner in the new business. She was a great recruiter and had great skills in the staffing industry and I believe we could have been a great team in our new business endeavors. Well, here comes my "pink slip" execution.

Believe me when I tell you, if you don't receive those "exploratory entrepreneurial nuggets" when they are given to you, you will be sorry that you didn't. Recognize them for your own entrepreneurial sake.

Well, eventually XYZ Staffing called me to corporate for a meeting. Now it's not unusual for corporate to call the managers and staff to meetings. In fact, I didn't have a clue why this meeting was being called because I never received the memo. HUH? Now I bet my friend and fellow colleague got the memo, what you think? Well, I was so busy that I kept rescheduling to meet because I had so many important scheduled appointments with clients for their business needs but I eventually got on their calendar and met with them all. I mean ALL of them. LOL!

But even during the last days of my "pink slip" departure that was scheduled to happen, I had been meeting with Pil Kim in solidifying my move to start the new business venture. He already had a contractual two year lease where I could immediately set up the business and get started. We met to discuss the particulars of which he and I came up with the name of the new staffing agency. WOW! Now, trust me when I share this with you, I had no clue he was just hiring me to run it. Remember in the interim of this story, he was "picking my brain" but he knew I was equipped to start this new staffing agency. So the contract stated I was the Vice President of my new staffing agency. It was my responsibility to run it. I was ready to do this in my mind but I wasn't ready to let go of my job. So I kept securing clients for XYZ Staffing agency and placing candidates on jobs while scheduling to meet with corporate. LOL!

Approximately two weeks of this process between working my current job and preparing in my mind when I was going to start this new business venture and waiting on meeting with Corporate about whatever they needed to meet with me about, all this came tumbling down and all at the same time.

I hadn't made a commitment as of yet to Pil Kim but the ball had gotten rolling on it. Trust me! I'm finally sitting in the boardroom of the XYZ Staffing Agency waiting to meet with executives and who would have ever thought it was my "day of reckoning" with this company that I worked so hard in sustaining clients, staffing candidates on job sites and running my office with the friend that I had positioned (now I know why) a great employment opportunity had come to fruition.

Well, "the pink slip theory" arrived. It was the CEO, COO, VP of Operations, Director of Staffing, etc. who all entered the room and greeted me so warmly and with smiles. I was like WOW!! I must have done something awesome for all of the "powers to be" to meet with me. RIGHT!

To wrap this segment up and get to the juicy stuff, the only reason my "pink slip theory" was told to me was of my *"misusage of the office telephones."* I was informed that I made too many calls outside of the realm of calls for the company. (Now just sit there and wrap this around your head. Quiet Please! A moment of silence needed! Okay, I'm back! OMG!)

"So we are gonna have to let you go. We need your phone, keys to the office and schedule a time with us to get your belongings out of the office." OH REALLY! Well, I looked at each and every one of them with a big ole smile on my face. WHY?

Lesson:
"Is there such a thing of an exit entrepreneurial strategy? If so, create yours ahead of time! Prepare ahead!

Chapter 3

Moving toward Xtraordinary

"What lies beneath? The experiential essence of entrepreneurial thinking

Here we are readers! The exciting news is I moved from being an employee to being an employer. Not quite, but the opportunity did arise and if I hadn't received that pink slip this transition of moving toward xtraordinary wouldn't have happened. I know more than ever now. Whoever knows what lies beneath? Well as an entrepreneur and with the spirit of it, you need to be aware.

I realize after the initial shock of being fired with no warning, positioned me to experience more of the essence of entrepreneurial thinking. Meaning, your mind has to be more focused on how to be more creative, come up with some better ideas in your entrepreneurial path and be ready to handle what lies ahead of you. This is speaking straight from the horse's mouth, herself. It's interesting to consider the difference economically between that time and now. I might not have pursued my own business if there'd been other employment.

So I finally made that big leap! I've decided now not to work for anybody but myself. Now I want to be my own boss of my own company...

On the other hand, I really had no choice, but to go ahead and solidify the contract with Pil Kim and get that new staffing agency up and running, even though I hadn't wanted to leave my job. I wanted to exit at my own time and when I was ready. Well, now I had to get ready for-real and build on this new business I now committed to start. Well, Pil Kim had other plans for me and for my skill's net worth.

Deciding to be an entrepreneur may be easy if it's in your heart and you are truly passionate about stepping out on faith, but **the transition from being a regular employee to a budding entrepreneur can be tough**.
There are many challenges and hurdles along the way that I truly endured but if you are willing to make it big on your own and be your own boss then you have to get the ball rolling and so I did. As I have stated, the transition from being an employee to entrepreneur can be a tough road ahead. You have to prepare yourself for the challenges that await you and so I continue to share my story of moving forward.

I eventually moved into my first staffing agency office in Euclid Ohio, along with Pil Kim and went to work. I'm very experienced in setting up new offices and buildings from the ground up. Me and my inspiring and encouraging husband, Charles got that office up and running in no time. Yes we did! I eventually started in the few weeks marketing to new clients, called current ones and started interviewing prospective candidates for jobs. It was such an exhilarating time for me, seeing this come to fruition so fast and so soon.

Now Here Comes the Ball Drop

In starting a business, you have to have your legitimate business name, company involvement, tax id, government agency licenses (if required), tax information and etc. in place. As you read earlier, I'm experienced in my craft, I positioned myself to learn my craft and know the ends and out of my industry, right?

Well, Pil Kim knew of that, that's why he approached me in going into business with him. I just knew with him running his own check cashing business he knew of the required elements of the industry we started. So, as I implemented the internal aspect of the business, now I'm addressing with him the external aspect of the business like funding, registration details of the business, accounting issues, etc.

I had gotten the business up and running and in need of a few minor details in securing placement of new candidates for current job openings but I need to have particular information to secure the business for any liability issues. My so called partner of our new staffing agency wanted me to do some illegal predatory staffing in conducting the affairs of the new business. See all he saw was the dollar amount in staffing and felt that I needed to do my part and he would do his.

Well, his part was not making sure we had funding and accountability of the company secured to hire and place new clients. He refused to make me knowledgeable of these pertinent details and I expressed my deep concerns of his lack of not understanding these procedures in moving forward. So, after ongoing conversations back and forth for over week if not more, I get a call from one of my clients that the office phones were disconnected. (What? Are You Serious?)

I immediately contact my partner to find out if this is true. He not only confirmed he disconnected the phones but he is breaching our contract to work together. (What? Okay, hold on to your seats readers! I'm having a true stark-raving fit about right now even as I'm writing this.)

I literally screamed. I mean I screamed with pure anger and demanded to know from him why and how come? Matter of fact, I remember hanging up the phone and going to his office to see him personally. I hadn't contacted my husband to tell him any of this yet because I needed to meet with Pil Kim first and get the real deal, the low-down, the reasoning behind this sudden unethical business decision that was absolutely in my world, unheard of to do.

For the sake of moving to being "xtraordinary" I will share that I found out that Pil Kim only contracted me as an employee...how about that? Making me the Vice-President was in print only. He didn't want me to know of his financials as well as creating and implementing this business under our name. (Okay, did you read what I wrote?)

If you remember, we both sat down and created the name for the Staffing Agency. So with him keeping much of the intricate details of the business away from me, I did my own due-diligence finally and found out that he incorporated and registered the business name in the State of Ohio under his name and made himself the sole incorporator of this new business. My name was no where listed as an incorporator, director, nothing. I was livid! I was fit to be tied! He literally and voluntarily lied about our business alliance and venture and shut the whole operation down. So now what do I do?

Lesson:
Remember to do your due-diligence in starting a business! Know who you're doing business with, always! Find out sooner than later!

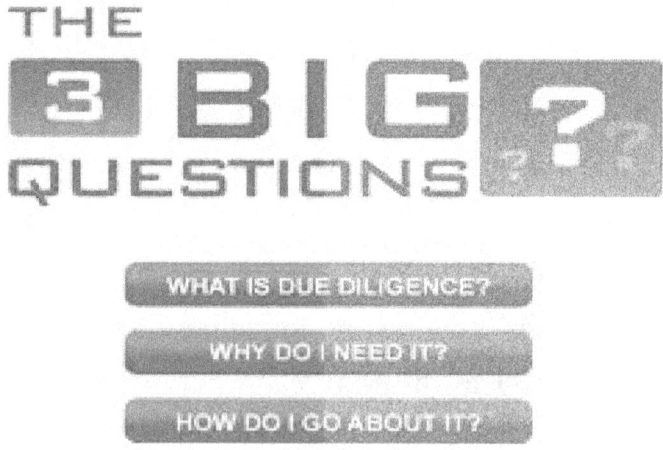

Due-Diligence is a term used for a number of concepts

involving either an investigation of a business or person prior to signing a contract, or an act with a certain standard of care. It can be a legal obligation, but the term will more commonly apply to voluntary investigations. A common example of due diligence in various industries is the process.

Chapter 4
Extraordinaire Beginnings

After getting sold out by my friend and fellow colleague for my job, then took the ultimate plunge and started a business of which I got hood-winked and bamboozled about the business. Now I'm back at ground zero. No job, no business and now about to loose my mind.

> *"Of course, if you have a large amount of capital you can hire people to do these things for you. But if not, you can always do things on your own. All you need is the willingness to learn how things are done and the patience to accomplish the task."*

So after I gathered my faculties and regrouped on what's next, what to do, how to go about it, what, what, what? My husband sat me down and we started brain-storming. Now this is so true. We weren't the whining – type of family now. He first brought it to my attention how I can retain and get back the business name that I implemented and created for me and Pil Kim. (Oh, I will share about Pil Kim and of what happened to his staffing agency later. HA!) Charles is truly a wise and brilliant entrepreneur and I'm not saying that because he was my husband. I'm saying that because he's the epitome of a true HERO....WOW!

We thought the business name out, until we re-created its uniqueness and came up with a great and better business name. He drove personally to the Secretary of State of Ohio in Columbus, Ohio and re-registered, reclaimed and revamped my original business name which is now called Labor U.S. of A. Employment Agency, Inc. This had to be the most exciting and awarding day of my extraordinaire beginnings. I saw my husband in such an eloquent way that day because he showed me how much he believed in me and the efforts that I was placing in becoming an entrepreneur, not just a business woman. Yes, this was truly my entrepreneur extraordinaire beginning. Thank you Big Guy!

Ready to Go the Extra Miles

Now its time to put the gears into motion and find office space, re-establish business relationships, network, network, network and start working on a business plan for my new business. Yes, mine! My mind was moving full steam ahead with great excitement because I had a great support system and now its time to start sharing about my new business and sustain clients and new candidates. I've been so used to following a work schedule so now I knew I better be ready for irregular working hours (this includes working during odd hours and losing some sleep). To this day it's like that. WOW!

In addition, I learned to make myself available to help new clients and customers anytime they needed me since it was just a startup business. Yes, it meant erratic sleeping hours, too. You may find this a bit difficult during the early stage but you will get use to it. I did.

See business people like Pil Kim have absolutely no clue how what he did to me, could have affected me, mentally and spiritually. Only the strong survive but it has nothing to with being strong. I had lost a lot in what had transpired, and if I hadn't had a trusting, loving and understanding husband, this could have been an internal or mental tragedy. Business folk need to be very careful on how they treat and conduct their business affairs and others.

Everything is considered impossible before it works. And, entrepreneurial thinking is all about doing what people say is impossible.

You couldn't have told me at this time I couldn't make this business happen. Oh no! After all that had transpired, I begged to differ. Many would have given up and found a job. Why? We are now getting into the nuts and bolts of what makes you extraordinary as an entrepreneur.

Entrepreneurial thinking is not just a passing fad and it does not lead to quick success. Oh NO! In order to be effective, the entrepreneurial spirit should be incorporated into goals, strategies and values of your business. Thinking like an entrepreneur enables you to stay ahead of others, whether it's your own business or anything else. Every individual has a varying perspective of what he considers to be useful.

First, it was all about the finding your niche. I believed I found mine. I'm a person of interest when it comes to helping people to get what they need. In this case it was employment opportunities. Seeking, searching and closing on deals with corporations that will hire hard-working individuals is what I portrayed to do and do it well. Being small and thinking big was my way to go because I needed to grow first before I could take on bigger challenges. I practice this creed to this day.

So now my generous husband assisted me with securing funding and I went head first into setting up and starting on my entrepreneurial path. Now I have formed my first and official office and proud of the direction I took in not giving up. It was truly a challenge to say the least because there were many staffing agencies like mine in the City of Cleveland but only one Labor U.S. of A. Employment Agency, that was my mantra and I stuck to it.

God blessed me with several new clients and I was able to put hard-working individuals to work. Business started growing immensely fast and I got out there and started networking day in and day out. As you all well know the importance of networking and I will share more about my speed networking synopsis later in the book.

Lesson:

Do you have a niche or something you love to do that will allow you to start and run a business successfully? Seek and find what your niche is and bring it to fruition.

Chapter 5 ➤

History of Being Extraordinaire

One who undertakes an endeavor is the meaning of the French word entrepreneur. It is really all about starting something and making it prosper while offering people the services and products they need.

I am in mere agreement of that statement above. Why? Because I too stepped out on faith and started something and became prosperous. As my first actual business was kicking off, I was finding myself doing more than just recruiting, screening, closing deals with clients, hiring, firing, placement, etc. It was becoming clear to me as I was out there in the neighborhood networking about my business, that many women like myself were interested in starting their own businesses too.

WOW! I mean, I would be interviewing candidates about future job opportunities and they would in turn compliment me on my business success and wanted me to share how I got started. Now it's a few years and several office locations later if I may say so myself with great excitement and these women and men were very open-minded about how I got started and it sparked their interest on starting their own. Unbelievable!

So on many, I mean many occasions I would be consulting about my entrepreneurial start instead of recruiting for job openings. Really, I caught myself doing a lot of consulting about business start ups and the how-to's. Now you can't make money for your business that way. My business required me to screen candidates for job openings, not be consulting about how to start a business. But I was doing what I felt was needed. Many of my candidates at that time resumes were so dynamic and show great leadership capabilities. In other words, they were hard to place candidates. Only because the economy at that time was truly re-structuring and businesses were laying off people left and right. So whatever positions that I was placing candidates in, the hiring managers most likely didn't even consider their resumes because of their highlighted accomplishments. They couldn't afford to pay them for what they were worth.

With that being said, I had to be creative and come up with other business services that would not only bring in revenue but help with supporting the needs of some of some individuals that benefit from my current services. I was already testing the waters with it, now I needed to make it happen. Now you know already from my early passages that I had received my paralegal certification in business law. It makes sense now more than ever to start my own small business consulting firm. So, now those entrepreneurial sparks are truly igniting.

Let me introduce to you now my second business endeavor, Wilder Consulting Business Services, now better known as Lamar Business Consulting Services, LLC.

Lesson:
Learn to re-ignite and differentiate your craft. If one of your products and services are not working, re-create and comprise your works. Build on what you already know!

You need to retain the aspect of thinking big while small because it is your very vision that will surpass what you currently do. The entrepreneurs of the twenty-first century have the advantage of coming into personal contact with their clients. This leads them to explaining the use of products and services more effectively. This is what I learned while recruiting for one business which opened up the mindset of starting another to solidify the need of the new one.

Most people have seen the history of entrepreneurship as a difficult thing to get into. This is for a reason because most business endeavors that are started will actually fail even without taking off. Therefore, there is great need to recognize this and to learn all the lessons that are vital for success. And one lesson is, understanding the mindset of being an entrepreneur. There are certain people that are known to have contributed to the popularity and emergence of entrepreneurship. You know of them, network with them, actually buy products and services from them. The history of what an entrepreneur is a *person willing to convert an idea into an innovation.*

From my standpoint in sharing all this is why my decision to become an entrepreneur and start a business was so unique. However, it should not be dependent upon the desire to become wealthy by any means. Instead, it should about being self-employed and managing your own business and/or developing your own personal dream. The history of it should be a personal choice that is based on a series of preferences or goals that one would like to achieve.

Also history shares that, very seldom does a great idea for a business or product come to us in a flash, but the best ideas are developed over time through extensive thought and research. For those who are thinking of starting their own business, it is important to spend the time needed learning from others in the field, other business owners and business experts, and entrepreneur extraordinaires as well as, thoroughly developing an effective business plan and other strategic methods.

As I continue to move toward the Extraordinaire aspect of this book, I'm elated about being in position to provide you some of my nuggets, yeah, that's the new seed word I now use during my travels and history in becoming an entrepreneur.

One of the top reasons for starting your own business is always opportunity. If you have ever had a great idea for a product or business, no doubt you have spent a great deal of time contemplating not only the feasibility of the idea itself, but also how to implement and the opportunities that this could provide for you and other people. Perhaps you have spent years in the corporate world or using your skills working for someone else and feel like you would like to advance your own ideas or products to realize the same dreams. Perhaps you are searching for independence or the opportunity to work closer to your family and exercise your own ideas and decision making skills. Well this is where the history of being extraordinary begins.

Lesson:

Do you have a legacy you want to leave? Your entrepreneurial experiences will provide you that opportunity.

Chapter 6

The Entrepreneur Extraordinaire Herself

First off, this entitlement "The Entrepreneur Extraordinaire" was blessed to me by an awesome entrepreneur and great male mentor friend of mine by the name of Cortes Everett from Cleveland, Ohio. Upon meeting him in the business world back in 2000, it will take him to tell you that story about our alliance, another chapter of my entrepreneurial path of how he came to bless me with this powerful entitlement of leadership and I have to be honest, I never received it until now! I truly appreciate his insight of my potential entrepreneurial spirit that he envisioned way back then. Cortes Everett and I are remarkably one of the few business male/female associates that have sustained professional business alliances together within this milestone for now over ten years.

The biggest change ever in entrepreneurship is occurring right now. For centuries men have led the entrepreneurial frontier. But, for a multitude of reasons it is changing. It's now the women's turn to be the leaders of entrepreneurship.

And now I stand in attention. Yes, as a self-made serial entrepreneur, I commend my efforts on setting the pavement in supporting the needs of many if not more after me to be all they can be. With tapping into some of the multi-level marketing businesses like Mary Kay, Gifting, Avon, Tupperware, It Works Global and now Organo Gold Coffee, much of these multi-level marketing businesses brought a lot of business education and services to my ongoing entrepreneurial journey.

As I became more and more successful as an entrepreneur in my business world, I start recognizing over 10 years ago that women entrepreneurs are natural collaborators and we love doing projects together. When we find like minded women who we like and think we can accomplish something with, by combining our talents, we do it and get it done. I saw that concept a long time ago and felt the need to tap into that source.

I have a collaborative spirit and my attitude reigns with women in such a collaborative way that fluently seen and considered unsavory when witnessed. What I was experiencing early in the game of becoming an Entrepreneur

Extraordinaire is that when women do the work that they love to do, they feel great when they can do it with other women. I also observed women in business are very passionate, determined, strong and dedicated individuals. It was also revealed that women are searching for alternatives to the normal nine to five grind. We have so many other life responsibilities, commitments and time constraints that sometimes entrepreneurial ventures becomes a best-fit situation for women and their families.

What I have endured as well in learning more about the needs of women entrepreneurs is that, we have dreams/passions and we want to fulfill them by starting businesses. Women often are relegated to roles of lesser authority in the corporate world. Starting a business from what was shared to me is a way to get ahead and fulfill those ambitions. I am truly a product of the process. I surrounded myself with mind-like entrepreneurs over the years that helped to teach me that having a dream is not an option but a responsibility. Fulfilling it is my destiny. We as women in business work harder and juggle more to get what we want. Our responsibility is to work together to share hardships and support. Have a dream and get ahead.

Upon my determination in researching more about women in business – as seen by nature or by cultural conditioning – we are generally more social creatures than our male counterparts. We congregate in groups more often for work, for familial duties, and for pleasure (heck, we even go to the bathroom in pairs!)

This behavior predisposes women to be more adept at building genuine, mutually beneficial relationships that aren't solely based on the idea of, "what's in it for me?" but instead, "what's going on with you, and how can I help?"

My ongoing research revealed that women entrepreneurs may be in the forefront because being an entrepreneur demands relationship thinking, not competitive thinking. Our goal is to form relationships with marketing people, distributors, manufacturers, and their colleagues, even those who seem to compete with them. Through these relationships, women have more people recommending them for future business opportunities, supporting them and cheering them on. If you're the only one up the ladder, there's no one to help you at the top, or to catch you when you fall. So with that, it came so, so clear to me.

I stepped out of my comfort zone and began searching for a much better opportunity to give back of what I was yearning for. I mean I heard about nonprofit organizations and knew of the needs of volunteering my time to give back to help others. So, what organization would be a great fit for me to join? What charitable contribution can I offer to an organization of my time and efforts of serving my community? Well amazingly enough, be careful for what you ask for.

With all of my hard-work, dedicated self-marketing, networking and social-gatherings in the Cleveland community, I was in receipt of a letter from the National Council of Negro Women, Inc. (Cuyahoga County Chapter) that was hosting their annual luncheon and that year's theme was "Women in Communication". I was selected in being honored for my articles that I written for the Cleveland Monitor Newspaper back in 1999-2001 in support of How to Interview Properly for Employment. It was an article in exchange for ads in support of Labor U.S. of A. Employment Agency. So when I got that letter, I was extremely shocked and elated. I was being honored amongst the elite communicators for the City of Cleveland which included those in radio, television, magazines and newspapers.

I said, "Who? Me?"

I was just a nobody trying to be a somebody in the world of entrepreneurship. It was such an honor and what happened was I got an opportunity to check out this wonderful organization whose mission was to support women and children in the city. I went to research more about this organization of which I found out was a national and international women's organization. It was founded by Mary McLeod Bethune and was passed on to a magnificent leader by the name of Dr. Dorothy J. Height. I was so excited and felt elevated. I said, "Look at God!" Look how he presented this opportunity to me and now I will move forward to see how this would be a great fit for me.

Well, not only was it a great fit but I was honored with some phenomenal women of the City of Cleveland including some new entrepreneurial friends that were in business for themselves.

I was in entrepreneurial heaven. Yes I was! I went to my first meeting and joined right away. The dynamic leader and President became one of my first of many mentors and I am so grateful to her for taking me underneath her wings to groom and nurture me in my brick and mortar of serving in what became my nonprofit entity. This allowed me the opportunity to become apart of what is now my legacy. I was such a dedicated and loyal member of that chapter and served in every capacity of the organization. I was learning so much about volunteering of my time even though I was very busy in my own business. I learned to prioritize and commit to serve the needs of others.

The National Council of Negro Women- Cuyahoga County Chapter gave me my wings and proudly allowed me to soar within the realms of this powerful organization. I loved the Membership Committee. I became one of the top-notched recruiting members of that chapter. Well, why wouldn't I? Look at the business industry I currently owned. I always brought at least three to five members to our monthly membership meetings every third Saturday for over six or seven years.

I eventually was voted as Membership Chairman for a few years then ran for Corresponding Secretary and then became a Board Member in Good Standing and then served on the board of Public Relations, which I was very good at. I definitely learned about fundraising and was voted as the

Chairman to host the same Annual Luncheon that I was once honored at in honor of the First Ladies of the Church in Cleveland, Ohio. I have to admit, it was much work involved but after years of being apart of this organization, I got to show what I learned proudly. It was a huge, huge success.

I truly love this organization and I felt a sense of belonging. That positioned me to join others and understand more about how to serve and be a servant in my community.

Lesson:
What organization have you joined? Do you give of your time to support others and give back to your community? What charitable contributions are you making?

A non-profit organization (NPO) is an organization whose primary objective is to support an issue or matter of private interest or public concern for non-commercial purposes. Nonprofits are often charities, churches or service organizations and may be involved in an innumerable range of areas relating to the arts, early childhood education, politics, religion, research, sports or some other endeavors.

So as I continued to serve and give of my time to my community with the National Council of Negro Women it occurred to me there was now a small group of Young Professional Women Entrepreneurs that were joining and I wanted to know how to form a local chapter of NCNW to support the organization more.

As I presented the opportunity to the board of interest and how it would benefit the growth of this local chapter, it was turned down. I didn't understand their reasoning because I was bringing in young and professional women entrepreneurs from my circle to join. I envisioned how we could support more programs and give back collectively as a local group as the professional women group but they rejected my offer.

So I was bit disappointed. I went back to the drawing board to educate and propose how can I utilize this group of professional women that was geared toward supporting and empowering more women in business, in giving back to their communities by offering mentoring, one on one consultations, training and grant opportunities for disadvantaged startup women businesses.

I commenced my research further, read so many books on nonprofit startups and came across a wonderful book called **SisterCEO**, *The Black Woman's Guide to Starting Your Own Business*, by author Cheryl Broussard. I read and re-read this book and gained so many resources on how I could start my own nonprofit organization. I even reached out and wrote the author herself and shared with her personally on how her book encouraged me to implement what is now, Women Entrepreneurs Of America, chartered in November 2002 in Cleveland, Ohio.

I mean, I was so inspired and felt so empowered to step out once again and start another business, this time a nonprofit entity. Cheryl Broussard did respond back and was delighted to know that her book affected my entrepreneurial journey into starting a nonprofit.

Once the organization was formed, Women Entrepreneurs of America hosted a book signing for Cheryl Broussard for her book, SisterCEO in the Waterloo Business District of Cleveland, Ohio, August of 2003. She flew in from California and she joined and become a Member of Women Entrepreneurs of America. How exciting was that!

With getting the chapter up and running, I was blessed to meet a few die hard supporters of me and my current businesses. I reached out to these women and shared of my need to help me implement this new nonprofit in Cleveland and get it structured like it should be in serving our community of women entrepreneurs. Those that I met with, and shared my entrepreneurial vision about Women Entrepreneurs of America welcomed the opportunity help me jumpstart this organization.

We started out by having one on one meetings at my house. I hosted "popcorn meetings". Everyone that knows me knows that I love popcorn. Then we started getting the word out about the purpose of this new nonprofit and suddenly, it was shared with me by a few of my constituents that I should host a Meet n' Greet for at least one hundred women of the Cleveland community, sharing about the organization Women Entrepreneurs of America and have a membership drive for recruitment. And sure 'nuff, this is where the life of the Entrepreneur Extraordinaire began.

Chapter 7 ➤

Networking Extraordinaire

Networking ~ /✻net✻w✻✻(r)k✻ŋ/

the *activity of meeting and talking to people to exchange information and advice about business or interests.*

Business Networking *is the process of establishing a mutually beneficial relationship with other business people and potential clients and/or customers.*

Notice that I don't say anything about meeting people in this definition above; the ever-increasing slew of business networking meet-and-greet events have given business networking a bad name. The key to true business networking is the establishment of a mutually beneficial relationship, and that's an incredibly rare event at the standard shake-hands-and-exchange-your-business-card events that are touted as business networking opportunities.

The purpose of business networking is to increase business revenue - one way or another. The thickening of the bottom line can be immediately apparent, as in developing a relationship with a new client, or develop over time, as in learning a new business skill.

The best business networking groups operate as exchanges of business information, ideas, and support. The most important skill for effective business networking is listening; focusing on how you can help the person you are listening to rather than on how he or she can help you is the first step to establishing a mutually beneficial relationship.

Well that brings to me why and how you are and can be a great Networking Extraordinaire like me! Meaning, nothing by mistake is ever evident that when two or more are joined together in His name magic can happen. I've seen and witnessed it with my own eyes for over ten years now and how to make the network for you is truly simple. I can see it from here but it seems to be challenging for many. So unfortunate!

I want to share that my networking and business networking came by no mistake when I stepped out on faith in the City of Cleveland, Ohio. To be honestly frank with you readers, I saw it as my duty and purpose to those that I come into contact with to be very effective in building my net worth of networks. Each and every event, meeting, social gathering that I ever attended or hosted was a huge success. You may ask why? Great question! The answer is I learned a lot about how to improve on my customer service skills through my business networking socially.

Before there was the extreme online social networking, I became connected with a few real networking gurus like Cleveland's own, James "Jim" Webb and Cortes Everett. We collectively joined forces and hit the town of Cleveland by getting involved with the "who's who" in the entrepreneurial community. It was evident that we were excited about meeting and forming new business alliances in sharing our current business status and needs. But we connected with many entrepreneurs who would normally not come to events like these in showcasing and promoting their businesses.

Jim Webb was truly an intricate key of my networking social environment for many years. I loved to watch how he'd canvass a room. He had such an award-winning persona and a great handshake too. But he specialized in getting connected with entrepreneurs. I really don't know if he knows of this but, he amazed me so much not only as a fellow business colleague, but a true nurturer in the world of entrepreneurship. He is an encourager in so many ways in business and a great listener.

He managed to always share his ideas and incorporated them in how he could assist you in his own way. To this, I've always saw him as a Master Networker and I appreciate what he offered to the many that came into contact with him, including me.

With Jim Webb and Cortes Everett by my side canvassing the social networking scenes in Cleveland, Ohio and surrounding area networking events, we managed to set the tone of what true entrepreneurs can accomplish in giving back in support of business networking one on one. Jim promoted his wonderful business of marketing to other businesses through an awesome business directory website. Cortes Everett promoted his craft which was assisting entrepreneurs to achieve their dreams, visions and missions as a motivational speaker and entrepreneurship coach. I was launching and promoting Women Entrepreneurs of America in recruiting prospective women entrepreneurs to join our nonprofit organization. We were a great networking force together and they embraced my presence extremely as a unit of one. For this I will always be grateful.

I found out with these guys by my side, that the ability to network is one of the most crucial skills any entrepreneur can have. How else will you meet the clients, constituents and other contacts necessary to grow your business? But what I did find out was that some entrepreneurs are put off by the idea of networking, thinking it requires a phony, glad-handing personality that oozes insincerity. Nothing could be farther from the truth.

Lesson:
Now I want you to think for just a moment. What does a good networker do? How does he or she act? What is his or her basic attitude?

You may decide, for example, that a good networker should be outgoing, sincere, friendly, and supportive, a good listener or someone who follows up and stays in touch. Well, to determine other skills, an effective networker needs simply to ask of themselves:
"How do I like to be treated? What kinds of people do I trust and consider good friends in doing business with?"

Now that you have an idea of what attributes a good networker should have, take an objective look at your own interactive abilities.

Lesson:
Do you consider yourself shy and regard networking groups as threatening? Do you tend to do all the talking in a conversation? Do you give other people referrals and ideas without a thought to your own personal gain? Can people count on your word? Are you a Networking Extraordinaire?

Chapter 8

Building Relationship Extraordinaire

Now we are getting to the real testing of the waters with this chapter and rightfully so because this chapter is a sensitive subject to me. It's one that I know a many of you reading this should understand clearly. If not, maybe reading of my struggles, triumphs and strategic comebacks of building relationships as an entrepreneur will help assist you with these delicate hurdles that you may come across like I did. But as you cross those hurdles and overcome them in forming these awesome and well needed relationships, you will feel a sense of accomplishment and see how your business will elevate and successfully exceed any expectations that you ever dreamed of.

You have to know first that when stepping out on your entrepreneurial journey that there's more to starting and running a business than just a transaction, right? Please tell me you are aware of this?

Building a business relationship helps you to establish a

bond. Some of your newfound customers are even willing to pay more for a product and/or service if they have a personal connection with you and your company. From a public relations (PR) perspective, building relationships is cost-effective because the only cost is your time. Did you get that? Let's see!

As you read of my start as a new entrepreneur, it wasn't all peaches and cream, no it wasn't. But as you read of my entrepreneurial saga, I was building relationships along the way. Some may have been for just a season, some were truly for a reason and there are those that are relationships for a lifetime.

Much of your business relationships start with your ability to learn how to form relationships internally. Meaning your life skills!

Meaning of Life Skills

Abilities for adaptive and positive behavior that enable individuals to deal effectively with the demands and challenges of everyday life. They represent the psycho-social skills that determine valued behavior and include reflective skills such as problem-solving and critical thinking, to personal skills such as self-awareness, and to interpersonal skills.

There are times in all of our lives when we are struggling with a decision, or making a change, or starting something new and we get stuck. Well in this case, stepping out to start a business like I did. I educated myself and was mentored by many in knowing that practicing life skills leads to qualities such as self-esteem, sociability and tolerance, to take action and generate change, and capabilities to have the freedom to decide what to do and who to be. Life skills are thus distinctly different from physical or perceptual motor skills, such as practical or health skills, as well as from livelihood skills, such as crafts, money management and entrepreneurial skills. So in understanding this, we need to have these intricate skills in place in taking your entrepreneurial journey on the road in building relationships.

I can speak very frankly on this subject because where I come from, Gary, Indiana, life skills for me was about surviving and getting in where I fit in to take care of three fatherless children. Yes, my parents taught me how to respect others and sent me to school to learn how to read and write. But there were some missing links to my life skills while growing up and sending me out to the world those skills were missing.

Some life skills you can't learn from a book. Many of us learned them from other sources. Some people are good and others may not be so good of life skill nuggets. We won't really get into those different kinds of life skill nuggets but know that as you step out to form a business and ready to build those relationships to help sustain your business, there are some of the true life skill attributes you need to have because your business opponents will and you need to have them too.

Lesson:
Are you willing to incorporate those relationship life skills tools to help build deep function- future businesses?

I feel confident in sharing those with you here because I too had to learn and incorporate them as I grew mentally, spiritually and physically on my entrepreneurial journey. Dealing with people is not an easy task when you are not equipped with the right personal tools to provide the needs of your clients and business colleagues. Just stepping out there buying pretty business cards, setting up those whistle and bell of websites and talking that talk and not walking that walk will not secure and retain those healthy business relationships. No, it won't! You have to start with building "YOU." I did and I'm still working on it. Believe me when I tell you it was fifteen years in the making. So as I list those personal life skills I've learned and incorporated them in my own entrepreneurial growth, I pray you will see these as tools in support of yours.

The most important amongst them are:

1. Self-ownership
2. Good listening behavior
3. Effective needs negotiation
4. Ability to stay in the present moment
5. Toleration of differences
6. On good behavior forever
7. Golden Silence
8. Non-reactivity
9. Ability to internalize and work through conflicts
10. Readiness to provide emotional support

I learned that in any relationship, there is going to be give-and-take situations and circumstances change, but you should also feel that, overall, your value is always important In my entrepreneurial growth, I learned to always be prepared. We all would like to think that "happily ever after" is our destiny and that our circumstances won't change because of negative things. So not true. It is important that you have an active understanding of who you are as an entrepreneur and your business. The "stick too-it-ness" mentality carries you along way.

One of the main issues with entrepreneurs is communication and how to disseminate it appropriately in doing business. A consistent inability to communicate concerns or issues when arise about you and your business shows that you are deferring your emotional well-being and happiness in order to avoid conflict with your business relationships. Examine why you are afraid to represent yourself in conflict management issues and look for ways to improve that situation. Trust me, I am working on this everyday in business.

Learn how to go for your goals you set and follow them through as humanly possible as you can. If you managed to step out, create, start and execute this new endeavor of a business, than you should have the ability to dream and plan its outcome and continue to work on your individual life skills in securing these endeavors. It will show and your business relationships will prosper because of its ability to move forward.

And this is truly one I've mastered over the years and seen it been proven when I practice what I preach. Learn to form some *"balance"* in your personal and business life. Oooo Wee, I already know!

In today's busy society of entrepreneurs, it is sometimes hard to take the time we need to relax, exercise or rejuvenate. Many of us is our own business, chief bottle washer, financial advisor, bookkeeper, social networker, consultant, tax preparer, etc. etc., etc. If this is the case, make sure you compromise and find the time from making all that money to keep yourself healthy and balanced. I am a victim of these circumstances, trust and believe me.

So, these are just a few of the ways you can assess and define your value and life skills in assisting you with forming those ongoing and future relationships. It will take some time but be proactive in incorporating them everyday. I still do and it works.

Lesson:

Do you have what it take to build healthy and long-term relationships as an entrepreneur? Will you start with building on your life skills daily?

Chapter 9

So Who Are They?

It takes with great pleasure to share this new and exciting book **Stories of An Entrepreneur Extraordinaire: Lessons of Madame Founder**, with some of the most exciting and extraordinary entrepreneurs that I know. I mean in their own right, they are the epitome of an Entrepreneur Extraordinaire because of their spirit of entrepreneurship. I felt the need to leave a chapter opened just for my readers to get some of their "entrepreneurial nuggets" published and than you can see why I'm the True Entrepreneur Extraordinaire because I rub elbows with these phenomenal individuals.

I truly feel everyone, regardless of where you are in your entrepreneurial journey, will benefit from the treasures of my journey in this book. I know it will allow you to go out there and conquer as an entrepreneur the seeds to sow into your business endeavors and give you skills to build a successful business and handle almost any situation with courage and strength.

Read some excerpts from some of my fellow constituents of their life entrepreneurial journey comments of Mentoring, Sisterhood, Support and Service.

HOW OLD are YOU, Really?

Some, may have stated, that "I'm or You're too old to change!"

OH, Really?

To me, life has and always will be about learning, searching, seeking, and adapting. Change is inevitable, you can either accept it, learn and adjust, or get left behind. I asked the heavenly Father, a long, long time ago, when I was about 10, to please always give me Wisdom, and knowledge, and help me to learn, and do better, when I learn. Through out my life, GOD has blessed me, to have been within the company of some very powerful people, as Mankind see, and acknowledges them to be.

Yolanda Lamar-Wilder is one of my friends and mentors and whenever I meet with her, or talk with her, I am gaining wisdom and knowledge, each and every time. I was in the company of many, Higher pro-filed people, I grew, and grew, with learning stuff, that I could/would have never learned, had I just "fit in" with the typical day-

have never learned, had I just "fit in" with the typical day-to-day jobs, and life of an average person and family man.

I have always been somewhat of a history buff. I love Historical places, and facts, even the ugly ones, so that learning of the history means I may be able to NOT repeat that stuff, if it were not good. Even if it were good, hopefully another way might be even better at solving whatever situation may have been there.

So, the moral of this writing is, if anyone you know is too old and set in their ways, to learn, or make changes, RUN, RUN, as fast as you can, in the other direction. Wisdom and Knowledge is never about what a person already knows, it is always about what a person is willing to learn from others, and challenge themselves, Individually to Give Love and Respect to another's point of View. Ultimately, GOD is no respecter of persons, and Loves us all, and HE may have just decided to give the other person an Epiphany, and Vision, which would never be revealed to you.

There is ONLY (1), ONE, who is all seeing and all knowing, and WE/I call HIM FATHER, GOD, to Some, and Many other names to Others; BUT whatever/whoever He is

Called, HE is STILL in Control!

Live, LOVE, Learn, Share, Respect, and Grow, Always!
Terry "the Warrior" Reece
Founder/Chairman/CEO
Reece Enterprises/Time Travel Network/Family Media Company/**TDM** Comics International
Honorary HERO
Detroit Chapter of Women Entrepreneurs of America

5 Tips for Productive Entrepreneurs

1. **Develop a "Too Easy" Mentality.** There is actually nothing that can stop you from achieving whatever you set your mind to accomplish. If you understand that everything on earth was created for you to enjoy, then life is too easy. The "TE" mentality keeps you on a path to evolving into a better you daily. For the Productive Entrepreneur everything is a task that helps them to understand all things are possible.

2. **Establish a Stellar Team.** Have you heard the adage it takes team work to make the dream work? Well it is absolutely true! Productive entrepreneurs understand that there is power in unity. Developing a stellar team is not an option; it's a must to remain effective. Productive entrepreneurs recognize that every team needs to have the proper components which produce success. A stellar team is a team that is comprised of the most qualified people in position. Seek out the experts and put them in place. Never allow loyalty to determine placement.

3. **Small Achievable Goals.** In every business there is a a need for effective communication. A rule of thumb for

effective communication is determined by feedback. Allowing your vision to be broken down into long and short term goals is an awesome tactic of productivity. Train, teach and develop your organization by setting small achievable goals.

4. **Build a Strong Collaborative Network.** As it is said "No man is an island" and that is why Productive Entrepreneurs build a collaborative networks. Unlike others, this type of network is active and engaging and its partners are reachable.

5. **Become a 21st Century Socialite.** Social media is the way of the 21st Century and the future. Your business growth and development is dependent upon your social media presence. Small businesses are able to expand and extend their reach globally simply by connecting, engaging and promoting their brand to their customers online. Productive entrepreneurs learn the social media game by becoming a student of it.

By: Dr. Vernet A. Joseph - America's #1 P³ Expert
HONORARY HERO MEMBER

J. Stevens & Associates, Lorra Brown/Owner Accounting Services

www.jstevensfs.com

I'm excited about all that is going on.

I want to thank you for your practical, no-nonsense advice, and your ability to connect with women on all levels. Your enthusiasm for your work, and for helping people help themselves, is evident to all. I can't sing your praises enough.

Her heartfelt and inspiring passion to the organization Women Entrepreneurs of America (WEA), her warmth and honesty is appreciated more than anything. I continue to receive positive feedback every time I speak about the Founder, Yolanda Lamar Wilder and Women Entrepreneurs of America, you have touched more women than you know. I'm glad that we share common sense philosophy and Thank you for exceeding my expectations.

Quote:

Prosperity Diva Facts:

Your thoughts are everything. They form your mindset, moods, attitudes and habits. One of the greatest skills needed is the ability to change and manage one's mindset. The first thing to understand is how your mindset forms in the first place, then it will change your money habits.

Essence Bleu, Wholistic Wellness & Beauty Practitioner
Massage Therapy, Skin Care, Nutrition Coaching
Newark, New Jersey

I use to think becoming a business owner was unattainable-WRONG! There are so many opportunities and support available IF YOU TRULY SEEK IT. Women Entrepreneurs of America offers PRICELESS business consulting, coaching, resources and more.

If you need help developing a business plan, obtaining grants, starting a non-profit, filing paperwork for 501 3 (c), W.E.A helps you with ALL of that. Although Yolanda Lamar-Wilder also offers these services through her for profit Lamar Business Consulting Services LLC, through her nonprofit, WEA, she offers the same services for only $65/YEAR!! Being an entrepreneur doesn't have to cost an arm and leg and WEA can show you how to make your dreams come true: STEP by STEP. I took a few steps back so Madame Founder, Yolanda Lamar-Wilder can help me LEAP FORWARD. Knowledge is POWER.

Quote:
"Live in balance: No matter how important success might seem to you, it is still important to follow it with balance; otherwise your journey towards success will turn into an

obsession that will ruin everything that you truly love in life. Success is not a destination. It's a journey, and it's important that we take each step feeling grounded and balanced. Spend time with your loved ones, enjoy your hobby or follow your passion, take care of your health and grow spiritually. This is the meaning of true success, the one that you can achieve only in balance.'

Wendy Lee, Dream Town Real Estate
The Ultimate Entrepreneur

Truly made an investment in my self and partnered with two influential entrepreneurial women, who have been dear friends, and mentors in my life. They helped me become the businesswoman that I am today!

Had to share these nuggets, from one of my WEA sisters....
I LOVE BEING UNCOMFORTABLE!

Stepping out of your comfort zone is UNCOMFORTABLE. You will not achieve your goals in life nor successfully follow your dreams in the comfort zone. The key is to make sure the "reward" is great enough and "Keep your eye on the prize." Stay focused. Today, take the RISK. Come and join me because I AM UNCOMFORTABLE!

Came to an epiphany, RISK COMES WITH REWARDS!!! with Yolanda Lamar Wilder.

Chapter 10
The Story of an Entrepreneurial Women's Organization

In November, 2002 I embarked on this entrepreneurial business journey called Women Entrepreneurs of America (WEA) without really having any idea what the path ahead would look like. The reason I implemented WEA was that I wanted to connect with local disadvantaged women in business of the Cleveland, Ohio community to learn from each other and to collaborate together and to learn from more *"mind-like"* entrepreneurs that are seasoned on business development topics and on startup businesses.

As we have embarked on the continued growth over the years of this nonprofit organization, I decided to turn around and look back at the long road that has led me to this spot right here and acknowledge what it took to get here. I really encourage you to do the same with your own entrepreneurial journey!

What I see when I look back is a road lined with the most amazing individuals that I've had the honor, blessing and privilege of connecting with for now 10 years. Also, I see the incredible leaders, business women, speakers, consultants and mentors that have helped to make this trip an enjoyable ride as starting out as an entrepreneur myself in 1999! It has been a windy path with many potholes and sharp turns, but I've learned so much and I know I am now such a completely different person than I was 10 years ago.

Also I know that when I now look ahead to the road in front of me, I will always continue to reach and give back to those that have assisted me along the way. Even if I can't see more than a few miles ahead of me, I do know that I'll continue to meet more amazing people. I'll continue to encounter and learn from the potholes and sharp turns and I'll be an even better person in another 10 years!

What's so incredible, there was never a thought of creating a national presence when I implemented the local chapter in Cleveland, Ohio. The goal was to serve the disadvantaged women entrepreneurs like myself of the Cleveland and surrounding communities. But what crept into our world was the "world wide web", internet, website, social networking online and it just grew wings and went south, north, east and west. Truth be told, the word got out about Women Entrepreneurs Of America and the interest sparked such an ignite about our service to women in business that women were emailing their request to start a local chapter of our mission in their communities. UNHEARD OF!

Seriously, members of the local chapter in Cleveland was sharing about our organization to their other business associates and colleagues and we were receiving requests to attend meetings of our local chapter for others to learn more about our purpose.

A phenomenal group of women from the Detroit community were the first to reach out to the WEA of Cleveland and attended our third Anniversary Membership Meeting in November of 2005 and their presence was so received. As they were departing and socializing, they requested to implement a local chapter in Detroit, Michigan and of course with me not having a clue on how to form a chapter of any kind for an organization, I said yes and let's make it happen. So, I went to work on researching and developing my craft as an entrepreneur in educating myself and seeking support of some veterans in the industry on how to form chapters for an organization and trust me, I went to work.

I connected with the future leaders of this first and I mean first ever for our organization individuals on a weekly basis of which we scheduled the first Meet n' Greet for our first Chapter of Women Entrepreneurs of America, introducing to you, January 2006, the Detroit Chapter of Women Entrepreneurs of America was chartered. Spearheaded by an awesome young lady by the name of Salena Jackson, we met at Sparkle Restaurant and held our first Membership Meeting of this New Chapter. Such a great feeling and those past Executives that joined me in Detroit was spirit filled like I am. Ms. Jackson had a meeting room filled of new perspective members who she had met and shared about this new organization and its need of a local chapter there in Detroit, Michigan.

The requirements to Start a WEA Chapter is to get at least *10 likeminded women* entrepreneurs to join, seek a location to host your monthly membership meetings, host various of fundraising and networking events in promoting your local chapter and seek funding in sustaining your chapter to provide programs in supporting women in transition, youth entrepreneurs and our re-entry initiatives. That's it and

That's All!

Well this whole concept truly grew and grew legs and ran away from us! I mean, more chapters are being implemented and I along with a few of my Fellow Executive Members, now we call Cleveland our National Headquarters, we're traveling and setting up global chapters yearly. We pretty much have blanketed the Midwest such as, Indianapolis, IN., St. Louis, MO., and Chicago, Ill. Then we were requested to head east to Philadelphia, Pennsylvania and then down south, Miami/Tampa, Florida and Atlanta, GA. Then we came to a stand still and start building WEA nationally. Breathe! Yes! Breathe! With eight chapters and a few affiliate chapters that were formed such as Muskegon, MI. and Flint, MI., there are so many ways we can look at this now knowing what you have read. Truth be told, I'm still in awe of it all to this day. Trust and believe me! Where has the time gone?

Then much of my personal life started happening from 2007-2009 like divorce, relocating, and caring for a very ill and gravely disabled Mom. Many had not a clue of my personal challenges but those that did embraced and assisted me with securing the growth of WEA as I endured my life challenges. Much of my business was sitting dormant along with some of the global chapters. I was focused on being the caregiver for my Mom after the results of her double amputation of legs and triple bypass in September 2007. I was left with such a grieving feeling of desertion of two of my for profit businesses and WEA. But my family comes first and God continues to give me the strength to handle it all.

With very limited family support, me and Momma went through this journey together but I continued to stay connected and focus on my businesses, a little at a time. Even though I was not mentally able, I was spiritually sustainable to do it. I love what I do, I love being an entrepreneur and my spirit of it would not let it go.

So to God be the Glory my dear readers, my Momma is doing much better and God blessed me to continue on with my businesses and provide me with my needs to move WEA forward. More women were joining WEA monthly and coming together in unity globally. Members are meeting, hosting events and fundraisers, networking and socializing both on and offline in support of Women Entrepreneurs of America. I was watching my vision and dream come to fruition in full circle now. OMG! What a sight to see!

The downtime I had during caring for my Mom gave me a chance to sit back and reflect and to captivate and rejuvenate my senses in securing the whole equation of now Women Entrepreneurs of America being truly a National women's organization. We are branding the conception of "empowering and supporting" disadvantaged women entrepreneurs. We are the epitome of entrepreneurial leaders within WEA that give back of our time to support those startups and growing entrepreneurs in their struggle of sustaining their businesses.

Now the breathe of life returned and God showed me nothing but favor in allowing me to get more involved in the expansion of WEA. So with that, I get an email from a young lady in Beaumont, Texas back in December, 2010 who I've connected and mentored on Facebook who showed great interest in starting a Chapter in her community. Now, I ain't ever heard of Beaumont, Texas before so here we go. But she was so adamant about have a local chapter in her community to support her local women entrepreneurs, how could I say no!

With that being said, she brought the concept to Houston, Texas and shared with a few of her fellow business colleagues in March of 2011 as she was preparing to learn how to serve and run of what will be known as the ninth chapter implemented. Well, it seems that the "powers to be" made her see the bigger picture of having it to be a chapter implemented in Houston, Texas. So amazingly enough, the launch of this New Chapter was planted and set to come to fruition in July, 2011 right in Pearland, Texas. So now we have the Texas Chapter of Women Entrepreneurs of America in place and within this last year, we were blessed to form another Affiliate Chapter, Northwest Indiana Chapter (Gary, IN.) of which is the hometown of the Founder and National President, yours truly. This definitely was one of my goals to bring my organization to my hometown to serve my fellow sister and brother entrepreneurs.

Now as we began this next transitional journey into the next 10 years of Women Entrepreneurs of America, many of you are aware that things are shifting a bit but please know these changes are designed to support you on a new level, to give you the ability to connect maybe less often, however, in greater quality! Why the changes, well, I personally and professionally realized many things are changing within the national and global expansion of WEA and expanding to other areas that are truly in need of changing. One of the main reasons is that many people began to perceive WEA as a social club or group and while socializing and networking is ongoing, it's when you get with a group of women in a room together we identify this issue and know that, truly this is not the main focus of WEA. The main focus of WEA is connection and business/personal development!

So, as WEA begins to shift things just a bit, many of you have decided to end your journey with WEA and please note WEA will miss you! WEA appreciate your membership and participation and WEA hopes you can look back and appreciate what WEA has given to you in your entrepreneurial life & business entity such as the connections, education, tools and support!

However, for those of you that are serious about building a successful business and living an outstanding entrepreneurial life, WEA wants to continue to give you the opportunity to learn, grow and connect to collaborate with other mind-liked sisters and brothers in business globally. Please know that WEA is here to support you along your amazing entrepreneurial journey.

About Women Entrepreneurs of America

Women Entrepreneurs of America is the nation's leading authority on empowering and supporting women run businesses. Founded in November, 2002, they have been assisting women entrepreneurs in starting and sustaining businesses across America.

In 2005, Women Entrepreneurs of America received national recognition for their landmark study of their Reentry Initiative Program, Project Return and in assisting women in transition. This study was responsible for exposing the harsh plight of America's reentry concerns of ex-offenders returning to the community. WEA has also developed programs aimed at identifying and offering solutions that work to assist startup businesses, reentry initiatives and youth mentoring.

Greetings from the **National and Global Chapters of Women Entrepreneurs of America (WEA)** and the *Founder and CEO, Yolanda Lamar-Wilder*! This year is a true milestone for all of us at WEA as we celebrate 10 years of leadership, sisterhood, support and service for and service to Women Entrepreneurs Of America nonprofit community globally. Implemented and Chartered November, 2002!

Now a decade down the road, WEA has grown tremendously from a promising idea among a few small business entrepreneurs of the Cleveland, Ohio community to one of the most successful and respected national women's associations in the country by far!

To honor this very special anniversary this year, we will host a variety of marketing and advertising events in the development and milestones about Women Entrepreneurs Of America growth. Kicking off in July, 2012 to August 2012, we will profile a number of the partnerships that have been and will continue to be so important to our success, tell the story of our members at work through words and pictures, and highlight our accomplishments and impact through the years. We hope that you get as much enjoyment out of turning the pages of growing as entrepreneurs as we did building the ongoing alliances that has supported the well-needed women's organization. It's truly an inspiring story of success implemented by an Inspiring Startup Entrepreneur and built upon tens of thousands of hours of brain-storming by many individuals-nonprofit leaders, program partners, investors and supporters, and WEA National and Local officers and board members to name a few.

Milestones are always an important time to look into the rear view mirror and reflect on the road behind us. Doing so helps to ensure that we are not only better prepared for future challenges, but more importantly, that we are well positioned to take advantage of the many opportunities that the future will present to us as now Entrepreneurs in the Making!

As we look back on the past ten years, there are three important factors that are fundamental drivers of WEA's success—our collective WEA voice expressed through our membership (now 650+ strong and growing), our commitment to excellence in supporting women in business and in all that we do as entrepreneurs, and our network of strategic partners that are aligned with our mission on a National presence. These three entrepreneurial drivers rise to the top and will continue to be the pillars of our foundation in the future.

Looking ahead to the next ten years, our mission to promote and empower more inspiring, disadvantage women entrepreneurs that are starting and sustaining businesses globally will remain the same and we will build upon our solid foundation of individual startups and seasoned focused member support to expand our work providing broader leadership for the nonprofit sector. Importantly, this will include expanded and targeted public education activities about the vital role of corporations and nonprofits and much deeper public policy engagement on the issues that will shape our future as a sector. We are well positioned to take this next step as a national women's organization. The best is yet to come.

We would like to close with a simple and heartfelt thank you to all of you—members, community leaders, program partners, and supporters—who have made Women Entrepreneurs Of America a shining example of what can be done when "women helping women to succeed" join together in common purpose for a better entrepreneurial future. We are *"tipping our hats off to you"* and God Bless you all for serving and being apart of the "entrepreneurial movement" with me and WEA.

WEA is a community of women who understand the demands of the entrepreneurial lifestyle. As one WEA member says, "WEA is an island of calm in a sea of stress."

About the Author
Yolanda Lamar-Wilder

Yolanda Lamar-Wilder is the Founder and National President of Women Entrepreneurs Of America, Inc., a 501©(3) nonprofit membership based women's organization that mission is to *"empower and support"* women in business and provide resources to those who want to start their businesses. She consults regularly with women-owned businesses from a variety of fields to help create synergistic solutions to world-impacting problems that addresses women in business. She is also CEO of Lamar Business Consulting Services, LLC. Born and raised in Gary, Indiana, Ms. Lamar-Wilder currently lives in Houston, TX after living in Cleveland, Ohio for over 10 years. She has 3 children, (two sons and one daughter), along with 11 grandchildren. Ms. Lamar-Wilder has honors with the National Council of Negro Women, Inc. and serves on several prominent national boards advocating the promotion of entrepreneurs of all genders and nationalities.

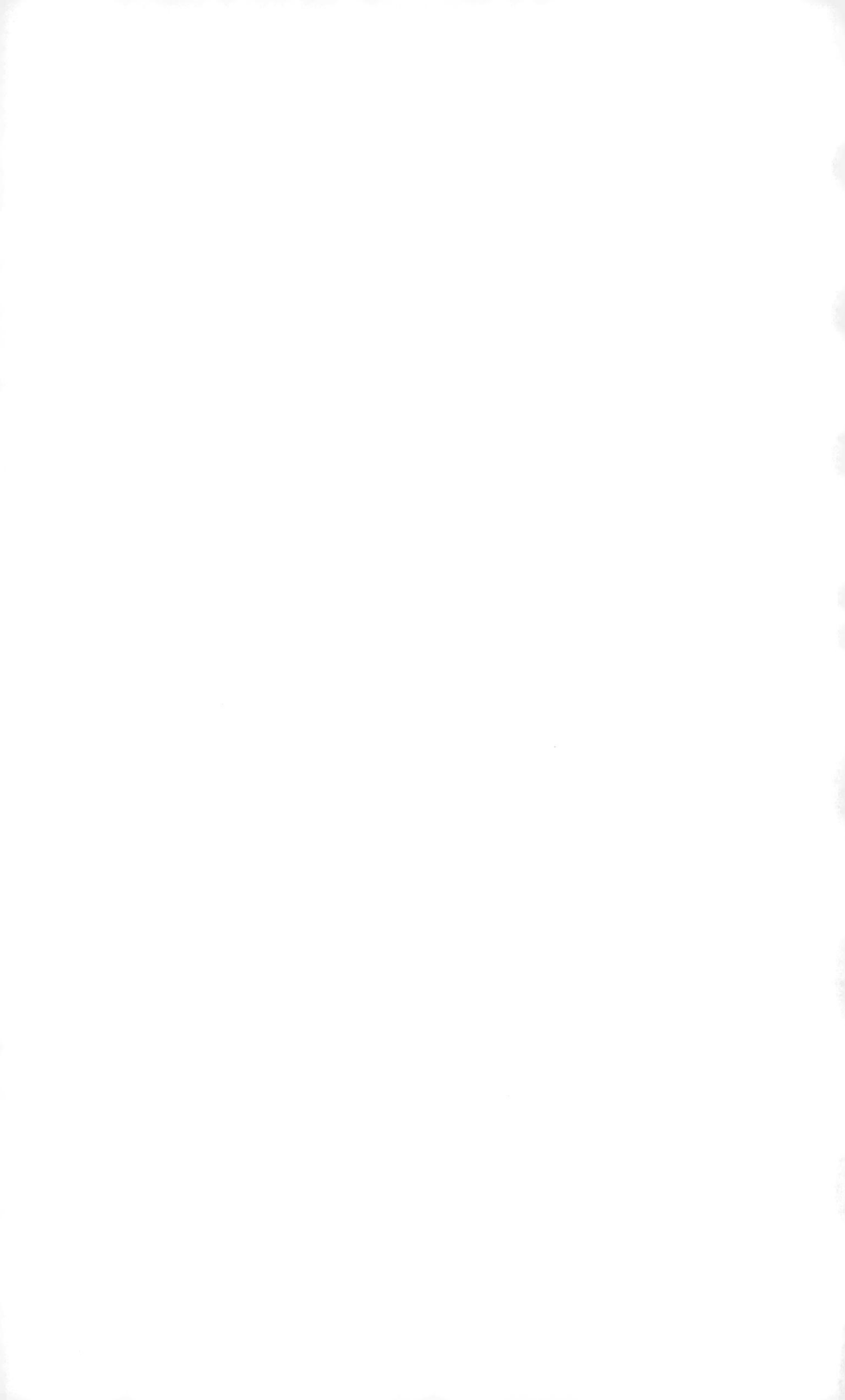

www.ingramcontent.com/pod-product-compliance
Lightning Source LLC
Chambersburg PA
CBHW061514180526
45171CB00001B/170